4.95

**fresh hope through**
New
Perspectives

CWR, Waverley Abbey House, Waverley Lane, Farnham, Surrey GU9 8EP

## National Distributors

### AUSTRALIA
Christian Marketing Pty Ltd.,
PO Box 519, Belmont, Victoria 3216
Tel: (052) 413 288

### CANADA
CMC Distribution Ltd.,
PO Box 7000, Niagara on the Lake,
Ontario LOS 1JO
Tel: 1-800-325-1297

### MALAYSIA
Salvation Book Centre (M),
Sdn. Bhd, 23 Jalan SS2/64,
Sea Park, 47300 Petaling Jaya, Selangor
Tel: (3) 7766411

### NEW ZEALAND
Christian Marketing NZ Ltd,
Private Bag,
Havelock North
Tel: 0508 535659 (toll free)

### NIGERIA
FBFM, Medium Housing Estate, Block 34, Flat 6,
Glover St., E.M., Lagos, PO Box 70952, Victoria Island
Tel: (01) 611160/866451

### REPUBLIC OF IRELAND
Scripture Union
40 Talbot Street, Dublin 1
Tel: (01) 8363764

### SINGAPORE
Alby Commercial Ent Pte Ltd.,
8 Kaki Bukit Road 2,
Ruby Warehouse Complex, No 04-38, Singapore 1441
Tel: (65) 741 0411

### SOUTH AFRICA
Struik Christian Books (Pty Ltd)
PO Box 193, Maitland 7405,
Cape Town
Tel: (021) 551 5900

### USA
CMC Distribution, PO Box 644,
Lewiston, New York 14092-0644
Tel: 1-800-325-1297

Coping with Long-term Illness Copyright © CWR 1995
Published 1995 by CWR
Cover design: CWR Design and Production
Design and typesetting: CWR Design and Production
Printed in Great Britain by Wace Archway, Poole
ISBN 1 85345 091 X

All rights reserved. No part of this publication may be reproduced, stored in a retrieval system, or transmitted, in any form or by any means, electronic, mechanical, photocopying, recording or otherwise, without the prior permission in writing of CWR.

Unless otherwise identified, all Scripture quotations in this publication are from the Holy Bible: New International Version (NIV). Copyright © 1973, 1978, 1984, International Bible Society.

# Coping with
# Long-term Illness

**Frank Gamble**

# Biography

Frank Gamble has served as pastor of a number of churches, now in the Community Church in Bourne End, where he has been for the last two years. He has suffered for the last eighteen years with a crippling arthritic disease that progressively attacks every joint in the body, and has been confined to a wheelchair for most of this time. He has been married for twenty-one years and has three grown up children.

I am greatly indebted to Joan Blunden, my personal secretary, someone who personally knows what it means to suffer from serious, life-threatening illness. She has patiently read my work on this book as I have written it, and typed it up for me. Her contribution has been invaluable.

**DAY 1**

# All For
# Your Good

> "In all things God works for the good of those who love him."
> Romans 8:28

In all things? Yes, in everything! As we encounter trials and difficulties in this life, we can be certain that God is working for the good of those who love Him.

Some years ago my specialist told me that the moment I was conceived, I was destined to suffer from the arthritic disease "ankylosing spondylitis". An unbeliever would call it fate. I've drawn the short straw it would seem, but as a Christian, I know from reading God's Word that God chose me before I was born (Ephesians 1:4). As I was being formed in my mother's womb the only true, living God knew me! What a mind blowing thought that is! He knew what life had in store for me, but He had already decided to draw me to Himself and make me alive in Christ.

I'm so glad that I'm saved! I'm so glad that my heavenly Father is in control of my life and watching over me with love and mercy. He is my refuge and my strength, my present help in the time of trouble! (Psalm 46:1).

God never intended anyone to experience sickness and suffering in this life. When He made the world, everything in it was good and lovely. It is sin which has brought suffering, pain and death. We live in a sinful world which, at this present time, is in the grip of the Evil One, who deceived man and tempted him to sin in the first place! (1 John 5:19). Don't blame God for your illness and suffering. God is totally good and righteous in all His ways and He is constantly working for the good of His children (Deuteronomy 32:4). Suffering shows us more clearly than anything else the nightmare of life without God. Many in this world are without God and without hope. As Christians we have a glorious and living hope.

Let me encourage you to trust in your heavenly Father. Satan will try to undermine your confidence in God; but don't let him do that! Keep yourself in God's love and when the circumstances of life appear to be going from bad to worse, remind yourself of this wonderful truth, that God is working for your good. He will change you and refine you during difficult times (Job 23:10). It is at those times also that you will come to know more deeply His love and joy.

The apostle Paul wrote to the Philippians and told them that God was at work in them both to will and to work for His good pleasure.

## For reflection and action

*Spend some time meditating on this truth and what it means for you.*

*Praise God continually for His goodness and ask Him to help you to live in the light of His Word.*

*Read and meditate on Psalm 103*

**DAY 2**

# Strength Within

"A man's spirit sustains him in sickness."
Proverbs 18:14a

Here is a vital truth to grasp for those of us who are suffering a long-term illness. It is strength within that will enable us to cope with sickness in our bodies. If your spirit is crushed or wounded, that is unbearable, no matter who you are (Proverbs 18:14b). You certainly cannot endure physical weakness and pain if you are wounded inside. But in our physical weakness God's strength can be made perfect. No wonder Asaph the psalmist could say: *"My flesh and my heart may fail, but God is the strength of my heart"* (Psalm 73:26). He knew a strength within his inner man that was supernatural, resulting from a close relationship with the living God. Being near to God is the best and most important thing for those who are enduring a long-term illness.

The apostle Paul prayed for those Christians he was serving in Ephesus to be strengthened within: *"I pray that out of his glorious riches he may strengthen you with power through his Spirit in your inner being, so that Christ may dwell in your hearts through faith"* (Ephesians 3:16–17).

What resources are there for God's children? We have immeasurable riches in Christ. We also have the best helper alongside us you could ever find – God the Holy Spirit. He is the One who strengthens us within. He also helps us to pray when we don't know what to say, and He even intercedes on our behalf before the throne of God (Romans 8:26, 27)

Prayer is a vital necessity for any believer, but I suggest it is even more vital when we are enduring suffering and sickness. You don't even have to worry about what to say because through His Spirit God has provided us with a precious gift that enables us to pray to God and, at the same time, be built up and strengthened spiritually (see 1 Corinthians 14:1–4 ).

Often when we are living with long-term illness, we can become preoccupied with our physical state. We spend more time worrying about our bodies than we do about our inner being. If you do that you will not cope very well. You need to make sure that you draw on God's strength within so that you not only "get by", but actually overcome through faith. Out of your weak body you can shine brilliantly for God's glory with a strong and pure spirit. A strong spirit will sustain you and it will cause you to keep a spiritual perspective on all that is happening to you. Spend time reading God's Word and praying, so that your spiritual life is constantly strengthened. Keep on being continually filled with the Holy Spirit (Ephesians 5:18) and, where possible, spend time with brothers and sisters in Christ, because there is a precious and vital strength imparted by fellowship.

The apostle Paul wrote to the Christians at Corinth and told them: *"But we have this treasure in jars of clay to show that this all-surpassing power is from God and not from us"* (2 Corinthians 4:7).

## For reflection and action

*Ask God to strengthen you in your inner being.*

*Adjust your thinking and lifestyle in line with the Word of God and live for His glory.*

*Read and meditate on 2 Corinthians 12:7–10.*

**DAY 3**

# An Act of
# the Will

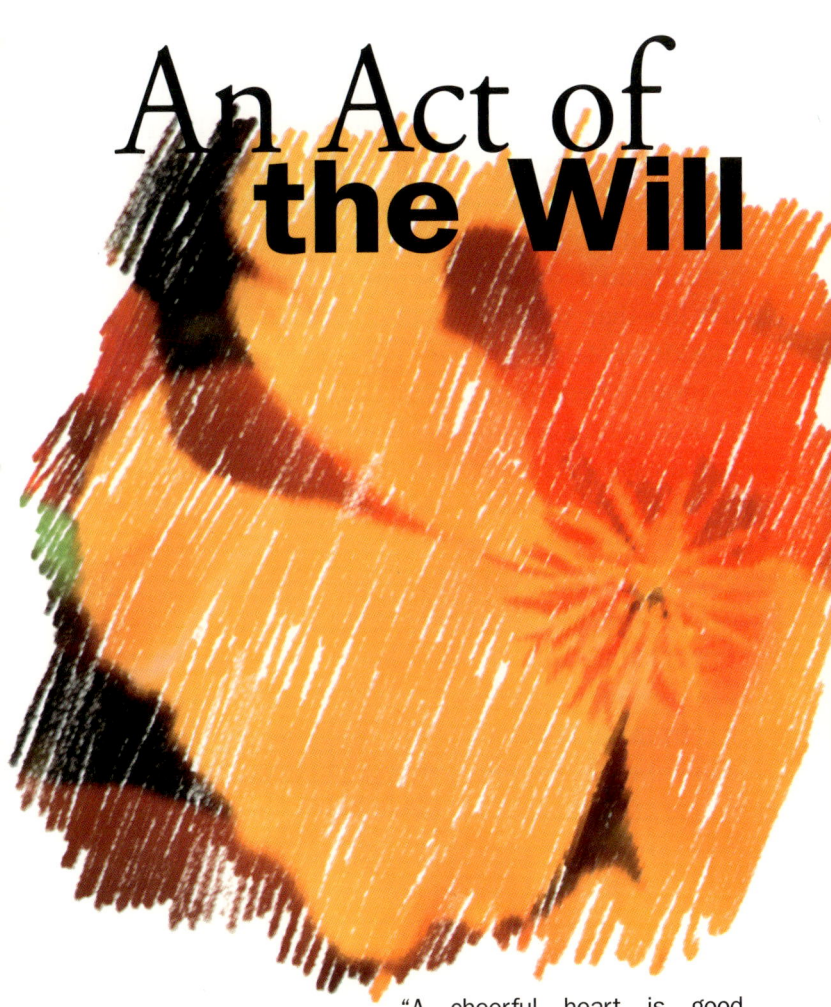

"A cheerful heart is good medicine." Proverbs 17:22

I don't know what kind of medication you are on, if any, but I can suggest some good medicine which won't have to be collected from the pharmacy! "A cheerful heart" will do you a lot of good!

Sometimes, being ill for a long time gets us into the daily habit of groaning and complaining. That is no good for us, and certainly no good for those who have to look after us. "Do everything without complaining" Paul wrote to the Philippians. It must be possible to actually do it, otherwise Scripture wouldn't tell us to live like that. We certainly don't want to end up being like Victor Meldrew of "One Foot in the Grave" do we?

Another benefit of having a cheerful heart is that you can enjoy a continual feast of God's provisions and blessings (see Proverbs 15:15). I know from personal experience that it is easy to know all this in theory, but very difficult to live it out in practice. My advice would be to aim at ridding yourself of bad habits and bad attitudes. Don't let unwholesome words come out of your mouth (Ephesians 4:29). Don't grumble and complain to yourself or to others. It is from our hearts that the springs of life flow; don't allow them to be polluted. It is also out of the abundance of the heart that our mouths speak; so a good heart will cause wholesome words to flow from our lips. Just think about our precious Saviour and the words that came from His lips. He is our example and our heavenly Father wants to make us just like His Son.

You may feel it is unreasonable to suggest that someone living with a long-term illness should be cheerful. Can we be in pain and still be cheerful? I believe we can. The Word of God tells us to rejoice in the Lord always (Philippians 4:4). If we are rejoicing in Him within our hearts then surely we can expect to be cheerful and not miserable!

I have been ill for over eighteen years now, but I know that it doesn't take much to remain cheerful, especially as we experience God's grace and the daily blessing of His presence. Being cheerful is, in reality, an act of the will. With a good heart and with the Lord's help, we can say "no" to grumpiness and complaining. Your cheerfulness will also be a wonderful testimony to others around you. No-one is impressed with grumbling and complaining, but cheerfulness speaks volumes about us as people and it will definitely bring glory to God.

One final word, to live like this will mean self-denial and self-giving. It is not the easy way, but we know that the narrow way that leads to life is hard, not easy! God loves cheerful givers, whether it's giving money or ourselves! You will be such a blessing and a channel of God's love and goodness!

## For reflection and action

*Ask God to change you if you have been someone who grumbles and complains.*

*Remember, God's grace is sufficient for us, so ask Him for grace to be cheerful in your heart.*

*Read and meditate on Nehemiah 8:9–12.*

**DAY 4**

# The Genuine Article

"We also rejoice in our sufferings ..." Romans 5:3

One of the results of being justified before God is that we rejoice in our sufferings. Even though I have suffered a lot of pain and discomfort over these past eighteen years, I have still been able to rejoice as a Christian. The apostle Paul told Christians to *"Rejoice in the Lord always"* (Philippians 4:4). Not sometimes, not just when things are going well, but all the time. The apostle James gives the same teaching (James 1:2).

It is important that we understand the true nature of Christian joy. Unlike happiness, it is something that is not dependent on circumstances. The prophet Habakkuk lists a large number of disasters but then adds, *"Yet I will rejoice in the Lord"* (Habakkuk 3:16–18). The apostle Paul brings out this paradox when writing to the church at Corinth. He tells them that he is sometimes sorrowful, but always rejoicing (2 Corinthians 6:10).

Notice that our rejoicing is *"in the Lord"*, not in the difficulties themselves. When the Bible talks about rejoicing in our sufferings, it means that we rejoice on account of the problems and the sickness, or whatever it is we are suffering. We do so because we know that something of spiritual and eternal value is being produced in our lives. We also know that God is for us and working for our good.

In this world we can expect trouble and persecution as we try to live godly lives (2 Timothy 3:12). We know that the whole world is in the grip of the Evil One, but through Him who loves us we are more than conquerors. Trials and difficulties test our faith, but when it is the genuine article it never gives up!

Perhaps your faith has been severely tested during your time of illness, you've struggled at times, you've known sorrow and pain, frustration and fear, but somehow you're still holding on, weak maybe, but not destroyed. Perplexed yes, but you've not given way to despair in your heart. One thing you can be absolutely certain of is the fact that your faith is genuine. You really are saved! Only genuine faith survives trials and suffering (1 Peter 1:7). Rejoice in this knowledge; rejoice that your name is written in the Book of Life.

Another cause for rejoicing is that through all that you have suffered you know that God has been refining you and changing you. Suffering produces the ability to persevere, and that in turn produces godly character in us (Romans 5:4).

I remember many years ago asking God to break me and melt me. I didn't fully realise what that would mean in practice, but I knew deep inside that I needed to change. For me to become like Jesus has required a lot of refining, and the process is still needing to continue now. How wonderful to know that God, our loving, heavenly Father, disciplines His children (Hebrews 12:6). My illness and the trials it has brought with it have proved to me the genuiness of my Father and my sonship.

## For reflection and action

*Remember that something of eternal value is being produced in your life through your suffering.*

*Read and meditate on Romans 5:1–5.*

**DAY 5**

# We
# Know
# in Part

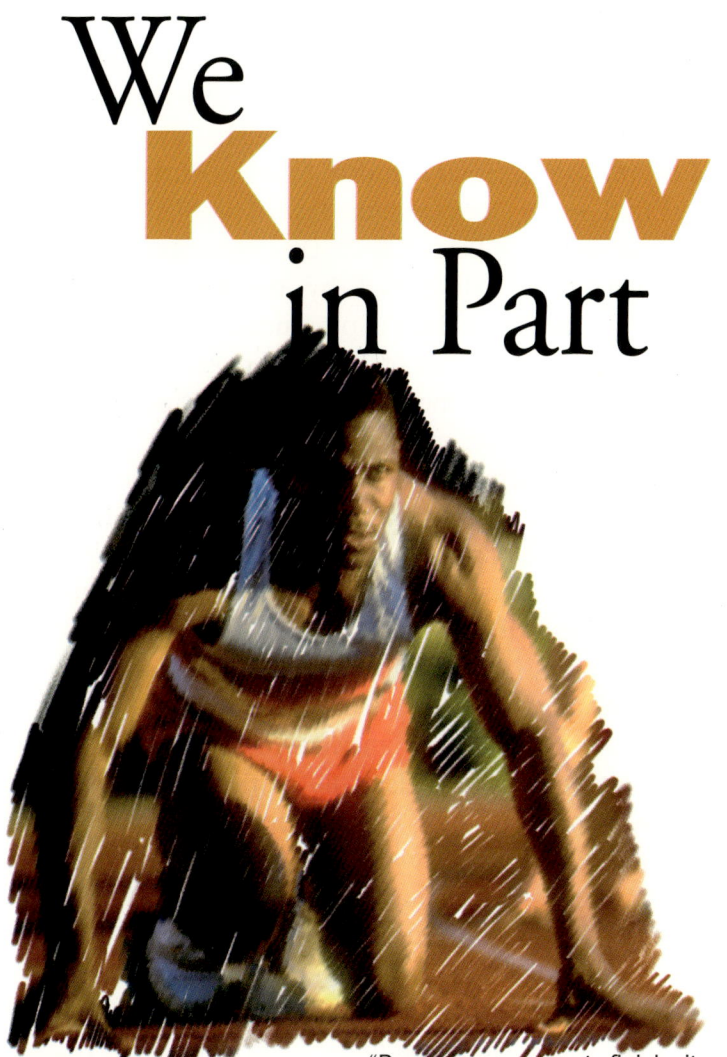

"Perseverance must finish its work so that you may be mature and complete." James 1:4

Suffering produces perseverance, the Bible says (Romans 5:3). It makes sense that ongoing trials and difficulties test our faith and produce in us the ability to persevere. According to James, perseverance itself has the effect of producing spiritual maturity in us as Christians. True faith never gives up in the face of problems and difficulties (see 1 Peter 1:6–7). On the contrary, its genuineness is established by the fact that it perseveres under all kinds of pressure.

A long-term illness tests faith as much as anything. Pain and frustration, the ordeal of daily routines, and just the sheer effort of trying to live life with some measure of fulfilment against all the odds, demands perseverance. Often we don't understand what God is doing. There seems to be no reason for what is happening. It is so discouraging when we pray and yet nothing seems to change. It is absolutely crushing when we pray and things get worse! What's it all about? What is going on?

I often haven't got any answers to my own questions, let alone anyone else's. But at times of uncertainty, we need to stand on truth about which we are certain. We know, for example, that God is working for our eternal good. We know that He loves us and that He has a purpose for our lives. He is at work in us, both to will and to work for His good pleasure (Philippians 2:13, AV). Right now we see only a little of what is happening, we understand only a part (1 Corinthians 13:12), but one day we shall know fully the reasons why God allowed us to go through specific experiences in this life.

One of the best examples of a man persevering under trial is Job. He didn't know what was going on in the heavenly realms but right at the beginning of the book of Job we are given an insight into the reasons why this righteous man suffered in the way he did. He was in the dark about the true issues surrounding his suffering. People let him down and it appeared that God had let him down too, but in the end things worked out wonderfully. Job did not give up and he never turned bitter against God. With patience he persevered and God blessed him more at the end of his life than he had at the beginning (Job 42:12 ff.).

Let me encourage you to read the story of Job. It is written down for our good so that we can learn from the truth it teaches and apply it to our daily lives.

Let me also remind you of our precious Lord Jesus who also endured incredible suffering (Hebrews 12:3). Don't give up! Don't listen to the lies of the devil, keep putting your confidence and trust in your wonderful and loving heavenly Father. Do you want to be mature as a Christian? Then you must learn to persevere! Do you want to lack nothing of spiritual value? Then you must persevere. God's grace is sufficient for us. *"Let us run with perseverance the race marked out for us. Let us fix our eyes on Jesus, the author and perfecter of our faith"* (Hebrews 12:1–2).

## For reflection and action

🕮 *Meditate on the quality of perseverance and ask God to strengthen you so that you can press on in Christ.*

🕮 *Read and meditate on James 5:7–12.*

**DAY 6**

# Never
# Alone

"I am the only one left ... ."

1 Kings 19:10

One of the worst things that can affect those of us enduring long illnesses is self-pity. Having overcome the prophets of Baal on Mount Carmel, the prophet Elijah is now overcome himself by the snare of self-pity. "I'm the only one left," he says to God, unaware that there are seven thousand people in Israel who have remained faithful.

Self-pity impairs our ability to think spiritually and, as a result, presents us with a dark and depressing perspective on life. Self-pity will always drag us down and ultimately lead to despair. We will be continually tempted to feel sorry for ourselves. Satan will make sure that we have constant reminders of how hard done by we are and how easy life is for people around us. He will ensure that doubts about God's love and goodness are put into our minds. He will also encourage us to be angry and to give up the fight as there is no point to it anyway. Of course, there is a point to it! We are fighting the good fight of faith (1 Timothy 6:12). We are living to please God and to do His will. God is for us and with us, we are not alone. There is "a great cloud of witnesses" watching from heaven as we run the race that is set before us. Our life will count for all eternity as we faithfully look to Jesus and run in His strength (Hebrews 12:1).

You need to be aware that self-pity will always put the focus on self instead of God. It will obscure His goodness like a cloud obscures the sun. You will lose your sense of destiny and the purpose of God if you start feeling sorry for yourself. My advice is to resist self-pity at all costs. If you entertain it for a moment it will do you harm. As soon as a hint of feeling sorry for yourself enters your mind, throw it out, fight it off, be ruthless with it!

Self-pity is like a burglar coming to your house that will rob you and mess up your life. Be on your guard. Don't leave any openings for it and remember that it will ultimately leave you in a worse state than it found you in.

A final word to those who have already succumbed to self-pity. Don't despair, God is able to rescue you from its clutches and He can restore you fully. You need to ask for God's forgiveness and for His grace to put it aside. Recognising it, and seeing it in its true colours is always the first step to breaking free from this wicked snare of the enemy. You will without doubt have been feeling low and dry spiritually, but from now on you will be able to walk in faith and be refreshed by peace and joy in the Holy Spirit. You will be free to embrace and rejoice in God's will for your life. As you reject self-pity, you can receive afresh the love of God and be confident that He *"is able to keep you from falling and to present you before his glorious presence without fault and with great joy"* (Jude v.24).

## For reflection and action

*Consider whether you have entertained thoughts of self-pity. If you have, deal ruthlessly with them.*

*Read and meditate on 1 Kings 19:1–18.*

**DAY 7**

# Steadfast Love

"Keep yourselves in God's love ..." Jude v.21

What a wonderful thing it is to know the love of God. What love the Father has lavished upon his children! Together we can glimpse something of the magnitude of God's love which goes far beyond our knowledge and understanding, and amazingly, it is in us that God's love is completed (1 John 4:17). The Bible says that God has poured His love into our hearts through the Holy Spirit (Romans 5:5). That has been my experience. I am severely disabled and over many years have experienced excruciating pain, but I feel so loved. I know deep in my heart that I am loved with an everlasting love, an unfailing constant love.

Do you feel loved? Actually, the truth is that whether you feel it or not, God loves you. If you are a child of God, you were predestined in love to be a member of God's family. God loved you before you came to know and love Him (1 John 4:19). It was out of His great love for you that He sent His Son, the Lord Jesus Christ, to lay down His life for you.

In a world where the true meaning of love has become blurred, we need to remind ourselves of what it actually is, says John, *"Jesus Christ laid down his life for us"* (1 John 3:16). It's amazing that the greatest demonstration of God's love is through suffering! You are loved, and nothing in all creation can separate you from the love of God (Romans 8:39). Your sickness, your pain, your suffering cannot separate you from that love. In fact, let me tell you that you can be more than a conqueror over your circumstances, not in your own strength but through Him who loved you from the beginning.

If the above is true, then why, you may ask, does Jude tell us to keep ourselves in the love of God? If nothing can separate us from God's love, it seems to be a contradiction to suggest that we could neglect to keep ourselves in that love. What does this mean?

If a person keeps plants, they have to make sure that they put them somewhere in the light. A plant needs light to stay healthy and to grow. In the same way, we need to make sure that we keep ourselves constantly in the good of God's love.

Some years ago, I used to wonder why it was that John the disciple seemed to be loved by Jesus more than all the others. Was he the favourite? It was a revelation to me to realise that Jesus loved all His disciples in the same way, but it was John who kept himself in the love of Jesus more than all the others. So much so that he became known as "the disciple whom Jesus loved" (John 21:20).

God doesn't have favourite children. He loves all His children in the same amazing way. His love is steadfast and strong, it will never change and it will never end. The Spirit will pour His love into your heart and will confirm and strengthen your hope in God, enabling you to overcome the trials and the sufferings of this present time.

## For reflection and action

*Make sure that, like John, you keep close to Jesus and soak up His love day by day.*

*Read and meditate on Romans 8:35–39.*

**Day 8**

# A Vital Lesson

"I have learned the secret of being content ... ."
Philippians 4:12

Facing day after day of illness and the disruption that it inevitably brings to our lives, can, and often does, lead to discontentment. We feel fed up, we wish that things were different and we allow our hearts to be troubled and resentful.

God's purpose for our lives is that we should become spiritually mature so that when our circumstances change our stability and faith are not affected. Paul faced changing circumstances. Sometimes he had very little, at other times he had plenty. From what he wrote about his life in his letters, we know that the apostle faced constant dangers, persecutions and hardships, and yet he could say that he was content and rejoicing in the Lord.

Notice, first of all, that Paul had "learned" to be content. It wasn't something which came naturally without a process of thinking things through and then working them out. He analysed his situation spiritually and not rationally. Rational thinking is never spiritual, it leaves a sovereign, wise God out of the equation. Paul learned to rule his emotions and his thinking, and this enabled him to stay content.

Notice, secondly, that Paul refers to this state of contentment as a "secret". People in the world are always looking for secrets: the secret to success; or maybe the secret to happiness; or even the secret to staying young looking. Being content as a child of God in any and every situation is a secret worth learning. Paul tells Timothy, in his first letter to him, that *"Godliness with contentment is great gain"* (1 Timothy 6:6). Nothing can compare with a godly life matched with the ability to remain content, whatever the circumstances. The writer of an old hymn spoke about life's changing scenes and said that in times of trouble, as well as times of joy, he would praise God.

Have you learned the secret of being content? Before you say "I could never be like that", you need to read what Paul also writes in the very next verse. *"I can do everything through him who gives me strength"* (Philippians 4:13). So God can enable us to be content even in the midst of difficult circumstances. Health or sickness, riches or poverty, even good and bad times, should not affect the way we live before God. A marriage can survive those changing circumstances so our relationship with God certainly should.

Being content will keep us from needless worry and wrong attitudes to people around us. Instead of our circumstances ruling our lives, we will, through God's strength, be ruling over them. Our heart will stay fixed and steady before God and our testimony will be seen in the very way that we live, whatever is happening to us.

## For reflection and action

*Learn the secret of being content and your circumstances will be kept in right perspective and in their place.*

*Read and meditate on 2 Corinthians 11:23–29.*

**DAY 9**

# The Strength of Your Life

"I can do everything through him who gives me strength."
Philippians 4:13

There has been a lot of emphasis put on "positive" thinking over recent years. Be positive about yourself, we are told, and you will succeed. However, positive thinking amounts to little more than convincing yourself to have a different attitude towards life and your own ability.

The Bible gives us an alternative kind of positive thinking. It has to do with having faith in God and His ability. As we face pain and discomfort it is vital that we put our trust in God and walk by faith, not by sight. When we are weak, our Lord gives us strength. When we are sad, He comforts us and lifts us up. When we have physical and material needs, the Lord is our provider.

Paul's faith in God's ability to provide for His children comes out in positive statements such as, *"My God will meet all your needs"* (Philippians 4:19). Heaven holds all the resources we could ever require and Paul, like King David, knew that all that we have materially comes from God (1 Chronicles 29:12).

Notice in today's text that Paul does not say, "I can do everything" and stops there, he adds "through Him". If he left those two words out he could be saying something totally different. It is through our Lord Jesus and the strength that He gives that Paul can do all things. He can't do all things on his own. It is not his own strength that he is relying on. He is not trying to release some mysterious inner strength that comes out of his own being, he is living by the power of God. The Holy Spirit has been given to us as our helper and teacher. It is by His power that we can live lives which glorify God and achieve the things which He has planned for us to do.

All of us, if we're honest, like to think that we can do things in our own strength. But in order to bear fruit that pleases God, we have to humbly come to the realisation that without Jesus we can do nothing! If you feel weak and inadequate then you are fully aware that you are incapable of achieving anything by yourself. But with God you can do all things! You can overcome fear and pain. You can beat the frustrations which taunt you and worry you day by day. You can resist self-pity, anger and bitterness. These things are possible through Him who strengthens you.

If you have been negative in your thinking, if you have given up trying to press on with God, let me encourage you to put your faith in an all-powerful God who is for you. In your weakness His strength can be made perfect. Your heart and your body may feel like giving up, but God can be the strength of your life (Psalm 73:26).

Isaiah shares with us a wonderful truth which the apostle Paul proved for himself, that those who wait for the Lord receive His strength in exchange for their own (Isaiah 40:31). Through Him we can soar like eagles over the mountain-like problems of life. Riding on the thermals of the Spirit we can achieve things far beyond our own ability or strength.

## For reflection and action

✢ *Remember the way you think will affect the way you live! So be positive, like Paul, and say, "I can do everything through Him who gives me strength."*

✢ *Read and meditate on Psalm 46.*

**DAY 10**

# Made For Better Things

"But our citizenship is in heaven."

Philippians 3:20

Heaven is God's dwelling place, the place where He reigns and where He alone is worshipped. The apostle John had a vision of heaven and the first thing he saw was God's majestic throne. The world may be in a mess, and evil may appear to be winning the day, but God is in control. He is reigning on a throne in heaven and His purposes and plans will be accomplished. One day our Lord Jesus will return in great glory and with the same power that enables Him to bring everything under His control, He will transform our bodies to be like His glorious body (1 Corinthians 15:52).

As you and I face suffering in this present time, we need to be assured that our God reigns. That is the truth! He is in control and working out His sovereign plan for the Church, His Bride. The Bible encourages us to set our minds *"on things above, where Christ is"* (Colossians 3:1, 2). We must grasp and focus our attention on the realities of heaven. You may be ill in bed; you may be in a wheelchair like me; or you may be mobile with great pain or difficulty; whatever the circumstances you are facing here on earth, your citizenship is in heaven!

Paul calls our suffering in this world, a "light momentary affliction", when it is compared to the glory of heaven. Whatever happens to us in this life, in this world, is nothing compared to the wonderful blessings that are to come! In heaven we will be free from pain and sorrow. In heaven there will be no death or unrighteousness. In heaven we will have perfect bodies and enjoy all the things that God has prepared for those who love Him. In this sinful world which is in the grip of the Evil One, we are bound to experience all the consequences of man's rebellion against God. These include sickness and suffering, and also a sense of frustration and despair in the hearts of those who were made for better things. Jesus came down to our world, but having overcome sin and death, He has ascended back to heaven. Your life on earth should now be lived in the light of all that Jesus accomplished.

## For reflection and action

*❧ During our time on earth, we are able to store up for ourselves treasure in heaven! (Matthew 6:20).*

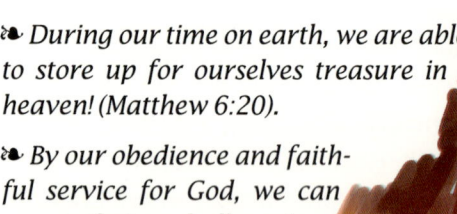

*❧ By our obedience and faithful service for God, we can ensure that we shall receive a reward from the King of heaven Himself.*

*❧ Read and meditate on Revelation 21:1–4.*

**DAY 11**

# Don't
# Worry!

"Each day has enough trouble of its own." Matthew 6:34

Jesus taught His disciples to live one day at a time. He told them not to worry about tomorrow and about their physical and material needs. Worry never achieves anything good. It doesn't change our circumstances and it certainly doesn't help them. Each day has enough trouble for us to cope with, without adding to it by worrying about what will happen tomorrow.

Face each day as it comes. Ask God for today's needs and be glad in the knowledge that He has made this day, and His grace will enable you to cope with it in every respect! *"This is the day the Lord has made,"* says the psalmist, *"let us rejoice and be glad in it"* (Psalm 118:24).

Instead of worrying about things, it is better to pray about them. As we pray about our needs and problems the peace of God will watch over our hearts and minds. Worry will be replaced by a childlike trust and we will be able to concentrate our attention on doing God's will and living for His glory.

I have often found myself worrying about my physical health and about things that could happen to me. This has made me very tense and fearful. For example, I worry about my breathing and my heart rate. I worry about my skin and pressure sores. I worry about getting colds and being knocked when I go to church. When you worry you lose your peace, and you can use up most of the limited resources of strength that you have. Worrying has not achieved anything in my situation and I have had to retrain myself not to be anxious or dominated by fear. I now try to follow Jesus' advice and live one day at a time. My heart rate has not bothered me recently and I am more cheerful and relaxed.

Are you anxious and fearful? Do you worry about tomorrow? A troubled heart will weigh you down and you will not be able to cope with your illness or the pain and frustration it brings. Ask God to take away any fear that is in your heart. His perfect love for you can drive out that unwanted burden. Don't be afraid to die because you are secure in God, and for any Christian death is gain.

I used to worry about dying myself, but God has given me tremendous peace and confidence concerning my eternal salvation. I had to meditate carefully on the truth of God's Word and what it teaches about death. I then came to realise that in God's sight the death of one of His children is very precious.

There is a time to be born, and a time to die. But we can live each day as it comes and trust God that by His grace we shall be ready when Jesus either comes back, or calls us to be with Him in glory!

## For reflection and action

*❧ Remember that each day has enough trouble of its own, so live a day at a time and keep rejoicing in the Lord!*

*❧ Read and meditate on Matthew 6:25–34.*

**DAY 12**

# No Comparison

"Our present sufferings are not worth comparing with the glory that will be revealed … ."
Romans 8:18

The Bible often puts suffering and glory together. Our suffering in the present is preparing us and shaping us for future glory. At the same time, the glory that awaits us enables us to cope with the suffering that we are experiencing now. It should be an enormous comfort to know that glory awaits you. When the apostle Paul uses that word "compare", it has two meanings. The first is to do with value. Comparing our present sufferings to glory is like comparing a toy watch to an expensive gold one. Secondly, it has to do with weight. Our suffering is like a feather compared to an elephant when you consider the glory of heaven.

As you experience pain and difficulty day by day, remember that there is a glorious, eternal inheritance waiting for you (1 Peter 1:4). You are being prepared for that future glory now by the things that are happening to you.

For many of us, this present time is all that we have. We live, we die and that is the end! How different it is for a Christian. We have been made alive spiritually through Jesus Christ our Lord, and we know that there is definitely a time to come which is much more important than this life. This present time will shortly end, but the time to come will be for ever and ever.

I personally would rather be saved and in a wheelchair, than be fully fit and on my way to hell. Compared to eternity, this life is very short. In addition I know that God has a purpose for my life and I am suffering according to His will. I shall therefore continue to do good and to commit my life to our faithful Creator.

Suffering in our body causes us to turn to God more and enables us to keep a right perspective on life in this world. We no longer live for evil human desires, but for the will of God (1 Peter 4:2). Our eyes are on the unseen things which are eternal and we know that we are following in the way that Jesus went.

*"And the God of all grace, who called you to his eternal glory in Christ, after you have suffered a little while, will himself restore you and make you strong, firm and steadfast. To him be the power for ever and ever. Amen"* (1 Peter 5:10–11).

## For reflection and action

᛫ *Let your suffering increase your desire for the glory to come, and let the glory that awaits you be a comfort to you as you live to please God.*

᛫ *Read and meditate on 2 Corinthians 4:16–18.*

**DAY 13**

# The GOD of Comfort

"We were under great pressure, far beyond our ability to endure, so that we despaired even of life." 2 Corinthians 1:8

Paul and his companions are very honest about the pressures they experienced in Christian ministry. They felt totally inadequate at times and life seemed hardly worth living.

Perhaps you have felt like that yourself, I certainly have. There are times when everything seems to be too much for us and, like the apostle and his friends, we can feel as if we have the "sentence of death" in our hearts. A long-term illness brings its own unique kind of pressure. At times we feel unable to go on, we haven't got the strength, the resources, or even the desire.

Why do these things happen to us? Paul gives us an answer to that question. He realised that these experiences were teaching him not to rely on himself, but on God (2 Corinthians 1:9). When we reach the end of our own resources it makes us depend on our heavenly Father. Paul set his hope on God to deliver him from danger and despair, not just once, but again and again.

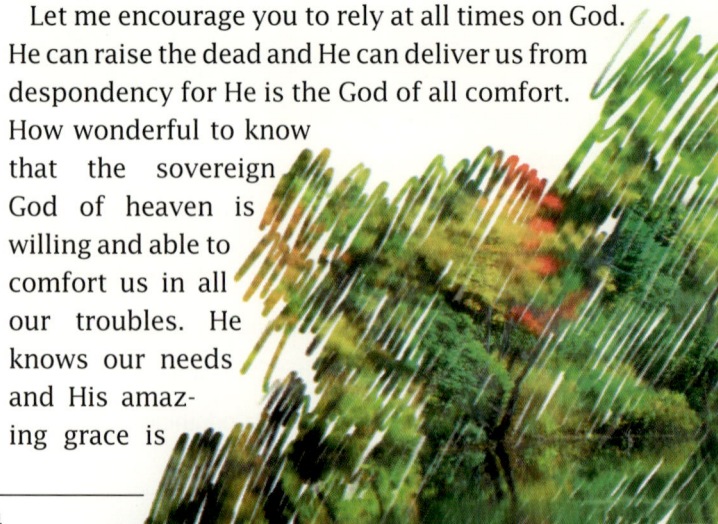

Let me encourage you to rely at all times on God. He can raise the dead and He can deliver us from despondency for He is the God of all comfort. How wonderful to know that the sovereign God of heaven is willing and able to comfort us in all our troubles. He knows our needs and His amazing grace is sufficient to meet them all (2 Corinthians 12:9).

It is incredible that in the midst of all the pressures our God can take us from the place of being in need ourselves, to a place of giving out to others. Having received God's comfort we can minister that same comfort to others. My own testimony is that having known God's grace and comfort in my own situation, I am able through Him to share what He has given me with others.

Just think, your suffering can result in you sharing with others! You can share what God has given you with those who are facing troubles and pressures without faith and hope (Hebrews 13:16). You can also encourage and strengthen brothers and sisters in Christ, some of whom may not be experiencing as much pain and suffering as you.

The God of all comfort can sustain you and use you for His glory. Be encouraged by this fact and don't underestimate your ability, in God, to minister to others.

## For reflection and action

- *Let the Lord use your weakness as a channel of His strength.*

- *Let your faith be seen in the way you act and speak, and let the comfort you have received overflow to people around you.*

- *Read and meditate on 2 Corinthians 1:3–7.*

## DAY 14
# Alert at All Times

"Your enemy the devil prowls around like a roaring lion looking for someone to devour"
1 Peter 5:8.

We must never forget that we are in a battle. We have an enemy who will attack us when we are weak and vulnerable. God's Word tells us not to be ignorant of his schemes and to stay alert and ready so that we will not become his prey.

Satan goes to and fro on the earth (Job 2:2) and looks for those whom he can deceive or defeat. There are various ways that he attacks us and we need to know what these are so that we can resist him.

From the outset let me assure you that He who is in you, our Lord Jesus Christ, is far greater and far more powerful than the devil (1 John 4:4). Our Saviour has already defeated Satan and there is no reason to fear him if we are living under God's rule. James tells us that as we submit to God and resist the devil, he will flee from us (James 4:7). John tells us, too, that the person born of God is safe and the Evil One cannot harm him (1 John 5:18). We must not be afraid, because fear is one of the things that Satan will try to use against us.

Another thing you must remember is that the devil is a liar (John 8:44). He will tell you that God doesn't love you. That's a lie! He will tell you that your prayers are meaningless. That's another lie! You must keep reading God's Word because that is the truth. The Holy Spirit will help you here and lead you into what is true and right (John 16:13; 17:17). Watch out for the lies of your enemy and resist him. The shield of faith is able to quench all the fiery darts of the Evil One (Ephesians 6:16; 1 Peter 5:9), so keep on believing God and His Word.

In my own experience, Satan has constantly harassed me during my illness with extra physical problems. It's amazing how one little additional problem can affect us. We feel discouraged and hard done by. Watch out for this subtle and horrible way of trying to drive us into despair. Keep your heart and mind clear of wrong attitudes towards God. Recognise what is happening in the heavenly realms and pray in the Spirit (Ephesians 6:18). The enemy wants you to give up and turn against your Father. Don't allow either of these things to happen.

When Jesus was on earth He had regular confrontations with the devil. On one occasion Satan used Peter, one of Jesus' best friends, to try and stop Him doing the Father's will. Don't reject any well-meaning person who gives you ungodly advice, but do reject the ungodly advice which comes from the enemy (Matthew 16:23).

Finally, make sure that you test everything according to Scripture and keep watching over your spiritual health.

## For reflection and action

*Don't be so pre-occupied with your physical state that you neglect yourself spiritually. Be self-controlled and alert, and then you will be ready when the enemy tries to come against you!*

*Read and meditate on 1 Peter 5:6–11.*

**DAY 15**

# Loving Discipline

"... but God disciplines us for our good, that we may share in his holiness." Hebrews 12:10

As God's children, we need to distinguish between spiritual attack from the devil and the loving discipline that comes from our perfect heavenly Father. Sometimes the two overlap, as with Paul's thorn in the flesh (2 Corinthians 12:7), but God always disciplines us for our good and with great love. He wants us to become like His Son, our Lord Jesus Christ, and in order for that to happen we need to change. Our Father can use the struggles of a long-term illness to discipline us and make us more holy. That's why the writer to the Hebrews says that it is for discipline that we have to endure hardship (Hebrews 12:7).

Be encouraged by the fact that if you truly are saved and a genuine child of God, you will experience God's discipline in your life (Hebrews 12:8). We need assurance about our salvation at the best of times, so take heart and rejoice that your heavenly Father is at work in you (Philippians 2:13).

There are two things that I suggest you must not do. First, do not treat this whole matter lightly. We must be willing to learn and to change. Secondly, don't lose heart. You may be tempted to give up, but although things are hard for the present you will eventually see fruit in your life, and this will bring glory to God and benefit to you (Hebrews 12:11).

In Psalm 119 David, the king of Israel, shares with us the spiritual benefit he received from God's discipline. It is clear from what he says, that he experienced times of affliction which caused him to change. He concludes that it was good for him to suffer, because it made him more obedient to God (Psalm

119:67, 71). He also recognised God's faithfulness in allowing those difficulties to come into his life (Psalm 119:75).

Because He loves you, the Lord will use what is happening to you to refine and teach you. Your character will be shaped and your heart will be made pure as a result of this heavenly discipline. In addition, you will also experience God's peace in your heart being confident that He is not punishing you or treating you unfairly, as is sometimes the case with human fathers. God's righteous character, His love and His justice, enable us to be sure that His dealings with us are for an eternal purpose.

I have personally arrived at a place of rest as far as my illness and severe disability are concerned. The Lord has enabled me to accept His dealings with me and He has been changing me little by little. I don't believe that I have some special dispensation to enable me to react in this way. Any child of God can come to this rest. I feel loved and valued by the Lord and I know for certain that I am saved. The work that He has started in me will one day be completed, and when in heaven I look back over my life on earth, I know that I will be able to say that He does all things well.

## For reflection and action

*Submit joyfully to your Father's training, knowing that it is for your good and for His glory.*

*Read and meditate on Hebrews 12:4–11.*

**DAY 16**

# A Changed Perspective

"But as for me, my feet had almost slipped ... ." Psalm 73:2

Psalm 73 has been a great help and comfort to me during my long years of illness. It is written by a man who shares honestly about himself during a time of immense difficulty (Psalm 73:14). He tells us that he was like a senseless animal before God and that he felt grieved and bitter.

There have been times when I have almost slipped while treading the Christian path. Like Asaph the psalmist, I have been perplexed about the things that have happened to me. I have seen people around me having a seemingly problem-free life while living for themselves, not for God. They seem to be affluent and experiencing no pain (Psalm 73:4, 5). Of course, we always see the things that seem to enlarge our own problems. Our perspective on life is affected by what is happening in our hearts. If we feel grieved and perplexed, we will notice the things of life that seem unfair and we can then become bitter. That's when we begin to lose our foothold spiritually and when we can unsettle other Christians by the things we say.

I am intrigued by the way Asaph got out of the mess he was in! Something changed his perspective on life. Suddenly his problems seemed to be less important. Instead of perplexity filling his heart, there was an overflow of praise to God! What changed this man's thinking? Basically, it was going to church (Psalm 73:17). When he went to God's house, he realised that there was a profound difference between him and the non-Christian people around him. He was on his way to heaven, but they were on their way to hell.

I'm sure that Asaph didn't take pleasure in the fact that the unrighteous were heading for judgment.

Such a reaction is unthinkable for someone who knows the grace of God in their life. But seeing life from a godly perspective did help this man to understand reality. After all, what is this life compared to eternity! He realised that God is not unjust, letting people get away with sin and selfishness. There was, after all, a point to living a righteous life (Psalm 73:13). He realised too that he wasn't on his own, God was very near to him. He would strengthen Asaph when his heart and flesh failed him (Psalm 73:26).

You and I need the same perspective on life that the psalmist had. Like him we should love God with all our heart so that He is our chief desire on earth. We should be secure in God's hands and allow Him to guide us through this life with our minds set on the glory to come (Psalm 73:24).

## For reflection and action

*As you face difficulty and pain, make the sovereign Lord your refuge and keep telling others of His goodness and faithfulness to all His people (Psalm 73:1).*

*Learn to enjoy His presence every day and to develop a godly understanding about life and eternity.*

*Read and meditate on Psalm 73.*

**DAY 17**

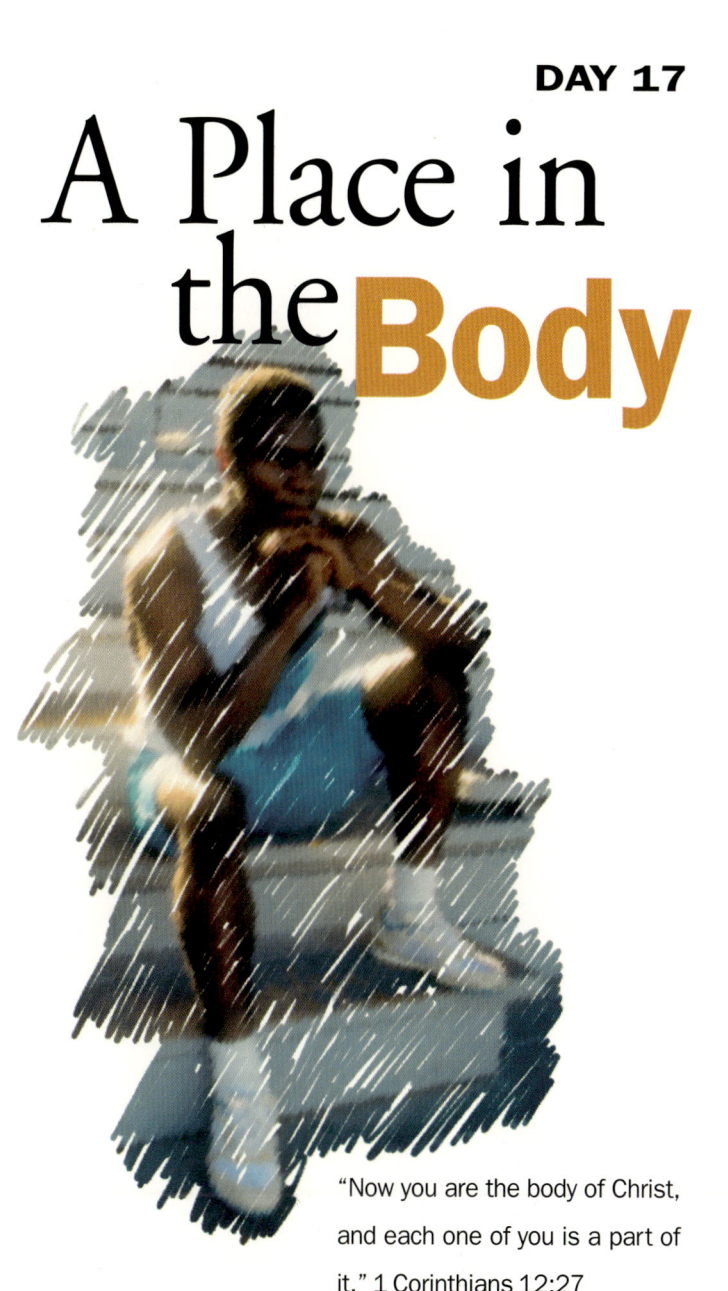

# A Place in the Body

"Now you are the body of Christ, and each one of you is a part of it." 1 Corinthians 12:27

55

As you face the struggles and problems of life, you need to know that God never intended you to go it alone! Christian fellowship is a vital and precious provision for all of us. Belonging to a local church is God's will for each of His children. We read in the book of Acts that when people were saved they were added to the church (Acts 2:47).

Becoming a member of a local church is not like being a member of a club, it is more like being part of the human body. Christians are joined together and are meant to be in close relationship to one another. It is very important that you know this truth and work it out in practice. We must not allow illness to prevent us from joining and being committed to a local expression of the body of Christ.

When Paul wrote to the church at Corinth, he described a wonderful unity and interdependence which ought to characterise normal church life. He says that Christians should be so closely knit together that when one person in the church suffers, everybody else ought to feel it deeply as well (1 Corinthians 12:26). I would encourage you to challenge graciously the people in your church to have that depth of fellowship and love.

It is true to say also that no Christian will ever come to maturity on their own. We need to be lovingly cared for and corrected by others who are going on with God. The interaction we have with brothers and sisters in Christ will sharpen us spiritually (Proverbs 27:17). There is also a vital need to receive oversight and godly wisdom from those in our local church who are called by God to serve as leaders (Hebrews 13:17).

You may be severely or partially restricted in the part you can play in church life but you still have a vital contribution to make. Don't allow Satan to isolate you or make you feel worthless. God can use you to bless and encourage other Christians. Your prayers, your testimony about God's grace, your giving, will all enrich the church to which you belong.

It's comforting and thrilling to know that Jesus is building His church in these days. God's manifold wisdom will be made known through the church and together God's people will be able to know, in part, the incredible and wonderful love of God.

## For reflection and action

*One day the Lord Jesus will return in great glory and then you will be with Him for ever.*

*The Bride is making herself ready for the coming Bridegroom and her God is working out His purposes. Don't miss out on the part that He has for you to play.*

*Read and meditate on 1 Corinthians 12:12–25.*

**DAY 18**

# Persistent
# Prayer

"Devote yourselves to prayer."
Colossians 4:2

One of the most important things for any Christian facing a long-term illness is prayer. Friends and family have constantly prayed for me; my church has prayed for me; and I have regularly prayed for myself. Prayer is essentially to do with our relationship to God. He is our heavenly Father, who watches over us all the time. He cares for us. He provides for our daily needs and His ears are open to our prayers. So we must regularly shut ourselves away with God as well as pray continually in the different situations we find ourselves in.

There are many people in the Bible who prayed to God and saw their prayers answered. Hannah was barren, unable to have children and feeling desperate. She cried out to God and He gave her Samuel. Elijah, who was a man just like us, prayed earnestly that it would not rain (James 5:17). He was devastated by the sin and idolatry in his nation and so he called upon God to show His power and righteous judgment against the wicked. His prayers were answered. There are many, many, examples of people like this who prayed when facing impossible situations, and God did incredible things for them.

However, we must remember too that there are times when prayers are not answered. Paul asked God to remove his thorn in the flesh, but his request was not granted (2 Corinthians 12:8, 9). David was aware that if he allowed sin to come into his life it could be a hindrance to his prayers. This teaches us that sometimes God, in His wisdom, does not give us what we ask for and that there are barriers to prayer. The Bible teaches us that lack of faith, wrong motives and sin can all hinder our prayers from being answered. So make sure that you deal with these things in your heart and be open to accept a refusal to your requests, or a delay. Sometimes God wants us to wait.

It is very important that we do not lose heart when we pray. Jesus taught His disciples to be persistent. We must keep on asking until God grants our requests or reveals that He has other plans (Matthew 7:7–8).

You may be asking for healing, for strength, or for patience. Whatever your prayers, remember that in all His dealings with you God is working for your good, and He knows best. It is not what you want that matters most, it is what He wants.

Here is the key to effective prayer. We can be confident that if we ask anything according to His will, the Lord will hear us and give us what we have asked for (1 John 5:14). This means that we need to know what God's will is for us, and that knowledge can only come by specific revelation through the Word and the Holy Spirit. If we don't know what His will is, then we must be open to whatever that may be and pray for it to be done. You may be weak and physically restricted, but you can pray, and those prayers will reach the throne of God in heaven.

## For reflection and action

*Be devoted to prayer and be persistent. Don't just pray for your own needs but also for the needs of others.*

*Pray for God's kingdom to come and for His will to be done on earth. Pray for those in authority and for our needy nation.*

*Read and meditate on Luke 18:1–8.*

**DAY 19**

# He Watches Over You

"The Lord is my shepherd ... ."
Psalm 23:1

David was an excellent shepherd. He knew what it meant to care for sheep. The shepherd would lead the flock to green pastures and suitable places to drink. He protected his flock and helped to restore their health when they were ill or injured. When wild animals came after the flock, he was willing to put his own life on the line. He was both good and faithful.

It is, therefore, very significant that David refers to God as his shepherd. The wonderful thing is that every believer can say the same thing. The Lord is your shepherd. He supplies your needs; He leads you and guides you; and He is able to restore you spiritually. You need to live in the light of this glorious fact every day.

Even if illness were to threaten our lives and we find ourselves walking through "the valley of the shadow of death", we need not be afraid. The reason is simple: He is with us, He comforts us, He holds us by His mighty hand, and we are secure in His love.

Jesus referred to Himself as the Good Shepherd. He loved us so much that He willingly laid down His life for us. He doesn't need to prove His love to us, neither does He need to prove His goodness and faithfulness.

As you face days of illness, you need to rest in those quiet places where the Lord leads you. Allow Him to feed you and refresh you spiritually. Allow Him to restore you when you feel weary or troubled. In the church God has given us those who will faithfully shepherd us and feed us from the Word of God, but in addition the Chief Shepherd Himself is daily watching over us. It is not right to say, "I don't need anyone else, I've got the Lord." Nor is it right to say, "I've got people to look after me, I don't need the Lord." God has provided faithful shepherds and He Himself watches over each of His sheep.

I once heard somebody say that goodness and mercy were like two sheepdogs. The Lord sends them to follow after us all the days of our life. We may face opposition from Satan but the Lord feeds us plentifully and His banner over us is love.

### For reflection and action

*Let the Good Shepherd anoint you daily with His Spirit, so that you can walk before Him with joy and strength. Rejoice in His faithfulness and love which will never fail.*

*Read and meditate on Psalm 23.*

**DAY 20**

# The Divine Purpose

"... we are more than conquerors through him who loved us."
Romans 8:37

Nowhere in the Bible does it say that life for God's people on earth will be easy. Actually the opposite is true, because it's clear that we will suffer in this world as we follow the Lord and try to live godly lives (John 16:33). What does it mean then to be conquerors? Will all our problems disappear? Certainly not. Neither will our lives be free from struggles and difficulties.

The reality is that, through our Lord Jesus we can endure troubles and continue to walk by faith. In the letter to the Hebrews we read about men and women who conquered by faith. They did not have problem-free lives. They were put to death, persecuted and imprisoned. They didn't even see the fulfilment of what God had promised concerning the new covenant. But Scripture declares that the world was not worthy of such people. They were more than conquerors through Him who loved them from the beginning.

Just think, the cross itself appears to be a place of failure and defeat, but we know that Jesus conquered sin and death. The cross speaks eternally of victory and the accomplishment of God's great plan of salvation (Revelation 3:21). In the same way, although our lives may seem to be full of suffering and spiritual battles, through Jesus they are counting for all eternity. The world would call us failures, but heaven declares that we are more than conquerors as we walk in the way our Saviour walked.

Being unwell for a long time is all about endurance, patience, struggles and frustrations. But there is another, glorious perspective on the same scene. A child of God is being changed from one degree of glory to another and a divine purpose is being worked out. There is faith, peace, joy and a growing certainty, not only about the future, but the present as well. There is a genuine and deepening relationship with the one, true God, and security in the knowledge that there is an unfailing, eternal love flowing from heaven.

Jesus tells the churches in the book of Revelation that He will give certain things to those who conquer. They will eat from the tree of life, receive hidden manna and a white stone with a new name written on it. They will have authority over the nations, be dressed in white, and be pillars in the temple of God (Revelation 2 & 3).

It is clear from all that the Bible says that this life is preparing us for the life to come. We shall receive a reward for what we have done and a crown of life from the One who reigns in heaven. This is the victory that has overcome the world, says John, even our faith (1 John 5:4).

## For reflection and action

*Let me encourage you to not only see your destiny as a child of God, but to work that out in practice with faith and hope.*

*Read and meditate on Hebrews 11:32–40.*

**DAY 21**

# The Real
## Issue

"There is ... a time to heal."
Ecclesiastes 3:3

From the moment I first knew that I had an incurable disease, I contemplated the possibility of being healed by God. Knowing God is able to heal is one thing, but there are many Christians who are sick and so there is a stark awareness that healing is not automatic or certain.

I found it very helpful to realise that there is a time and purpose for everything under heaven. God has a plan for each of His children's lives which is unique and special (Philippians 3:12). There is a time to heal, just as there is a time to be born again. That is not to say that there is a time for everyone to be healed, but if it is God's will for that individual, He will bring it to pass.

After receiving a number of prophecies and visions, I truly believe in my heart that God wants to heal me. But my healing has strangely become less and less vital as the years have gone by. Not because I have less faith, or I'm losing heart, but because my desire to live for God's glory has grown more and more (1 Corinthians 10:31). The issue isn't now whether or not I am physically restored, but rather am I obeying God and serving His purposes? I attribute this change totally and utterly to His amazing grace. So be encouraged, because if God can do this in my heart, He can do it in anybody's.

It is vital for you to know God's will with regard to your illness. You need revelation which is specific and well-tested by the Word of God. The Holy Spirit can make known to us what it is God wants, and He will also help us to have wisdom as we work that through in our lives. The Lord's will is always good, acceptable and perfect, and His timing is never bad either (Romans 12:2).

Make sure that you test everything so that you can distinguish between what is true and what is false (1 John 4:1). Prophecy needs to be weighed and our own feelings need to be under godly control. There is a safety in sharing with others who are obeying God (Proverbs 11:14). Be quick to hear the Lord, but don't speak before you are sure about what He is really saying.

Our desires must always come second to His desires. Jesus must have first place in our affections and lives. He must increase and we must decrease (John 3:30). If it is His will to heal, then we can praise and glorify Him with our being. If it isn't, we can still praise and glorify Him!

## For reflection and action

*When Daniel's friends were put into the fiery furnace, they said that whatever happened, they would serve God and stay faithful to Him (Daniel 3:17–18). Let us have the same attitude about our illness, whether we are healed or not.*

*Read and meditate on Ecclesiastes 3:1–8.*

# DAY 22
# No Accident

"All the days ordained for me were written in your book before one of them came to be."
Psalm 139:16

We are not victims of fate or circumstance. As God's children, we can be confident that each day we live on this earth is one that has been planned before the beginning of time. Our Lord Jesus has got a book in heaven and the name of every Christian written in it. That's why, when He was on earth, Jesus encouraged His disciples to rejoice in this fact (Luke 10:20). Even compared to seeing manifestations of God's power and authority, it is more thrilling and more wonderful to know that our names are in the Lamb's Book of Life (Revelation 13:8).

Before we were born, God chose us, in love, to be His precious children (Ephesians 1:4). He knew us and watched over us, even when we were being formed in our mother's womb (Psalm 139:13). It is very difficult to understand such things; God's wisdom and knowledge are far beyond comprehension, but the Bible assures us that this is true.

God told Jeremiah that He knew him before his birth (Jeremiah 1:5). David was convinced that he, too, was known and loved before he came onto the scene of this world. The glorious truth is that God knew you before you were born. Your life was planned and it was no accident that you became a believer.

Many people in the world today have no sense of destiny and purpose in life. But you and I can say that we know where we came from and where we are going. We can answer that heart searching question, "Who am I?" We can be secure in the knowledge that our heavenly Father loved us and wanted us before the world was made.

What a difference all of this makes to our lives from day to day – whatever life may throw at us, whatever hardship or suffering we experience, God is in control. He is shaping us for glory, and our times are in His hands. Our destiny eradicates the fear and questioning that would otherwise dominate our thoughts and feelings. To know that we are where God wants us to be, and that He has allowed us to be ill, does enable us to rest in Him.

The Lord has His reasons for everything that happens to us. We may not understand the reason now, but one day we will. The journey may be hard and full of danger, but knowing that we will reach our destination is the most vital thing. We can be certain that we are on course for future glory and blessing.

Jesus has lived life on this earth and He understands fully what we are going through. He experienced suffering and pain. He has gone through times of grief and sorrow. But knowing where He came from and where He was going made all the difference to His life (John 13:3). He could serve others freely and entrust Himself to the will of the Father. You and I must do the same.

## For reflection and action

*Knowing that your birth was no accident, and where you are ultimately headed, entrust yourself afresh to the will of your Father in heaven.*

*Read and meditate on Psalm 139:1–18.*

**DAY 23**

# Light on a
# Dark Path

"Your word is a lamp to my feet and a light for my path." Psalm 119:105

When walking in the dark, it is easy to stumble or fall. Having a torch makes all the difference. Not only can we see where the path is, but we can also avoid holes and obstacles.

A long-term illness, as I well know, is like a dark path. For this reason, we desperately need light if we are going to find our way forward in the darkness. There are many dangers that need to be avoided. Our hearts and minds need revelation of truth to enable us to walk along the path of life with confidence and safety (Psalm 119:169).

The good news is that God's Word is like a torch. It will show us the way ahead; it will keep us from stumbling or tripping up; and it will allow our feet to stay on solid ground (Psalm 119:133).

When we are confused or perplexed about what is happening in our lives, we need truth and understanding. It is at such times that God's Word can light up our path. As we read the Bible, we will gain insights into the struggles of life and into things which raise searching and profound questions.

It is good to read about men and women of faith who experienced many of the problems and difficulties that we face day by day. I have found great comfort through reading the book of Psalms. The honesty and openness that comes from the men who wrote them is a resource for every Christian. We can identify with their inner feelings, their perplexity and their heartfelt cries.

All that is written in Scripture is God-breathed, and useful for teaching and training in spiritual things (2

Timothy 3:16). In addition, the Holy Spirit Himself will teach us through the Word and bring revelation to our hearts which will cause us to grow and mature.

Don't allow yourself to neglect God's Word (Psalm 119:16). Be determined to read it and to soak up its truth. You will need to be disciplined in order to regularly study and meditate on it. Many people today read Christian magazines and listen to tapes without referring to the Bible. We must certainly use all the resources that are available for us, but the reading of Scripture needs to be a priority.

Let God's Word dwell in your heart richly (Colossians 3:16). You may not always feel immediately blessed, but it will strengthen you and do you good. Don't lose heart if it is hard going, because if you persevere you will reap great benefits. Like a two-edged sword, God's Word will reveal attitudes and motives that need to be dealt with (Hebrews 4:12). Like honey, it will taste sweet and wholesome as you feed on it (Psalm 119:103). Its truth will keep you from sin, and build you up spiritually. Finally, in a world where things quickly pass away, what a comfort it is to know that God's Word will last for ever (1 Peter 1:25).

### For reflection and action

*Build your life on solid rock by hearing and doing what God's Word says.*

*Read and meditate on Psalm 119:1–16.*

# DAY 24
# Continual Praise

"Through Jesus, therefore, let us continually offer to God a sacrifice of praise … ."
Hebrews 13: 15

It seems easy to praise God when things are going well, but what about when life is hard? Does God expect us to praise Him then?

The Word of God has a lot to say about praise and worship. It constantly reminds us that the Lord is worthy to receive our love and adoration. It tells us that we can enter His gates with thanksgiving and His courts with praise. It also teaches us that, whatever our circumstances, we can offer to God glory and honour. The truth is that even when we are sick we can worship the Lord. When life is terrible and there seems to be no way out of our troubles and suffering, we can offer praise to God.

Such action clearly costs a lot, but it pleases the Father's heart. We ourselves value things by what they cost. When people we love make sacrifices for us, doesn't that mean more than words can say? Surely then, we should not give things to the Lord that don't cost us anything! What a joy and delight it must be for Him to receive praise that comes from a sick-bed, or a wheelchair. How precious to receive devotion which is costly. This is what it means to offer a sacrifice of praise. We are a royal priesthood who offer spiritual sacrifices (1 Peter 2:5).

Notice that we are exhorted by the writer to the Hebrews to continually offer praise to God. David declares that he will do just that; his mouth was full of praise to God all the time (Psalm 34:1). You and I need to take this to heart. What a difference it makes to our lives when we focus all our attention on the Lord. We can rejoice in Him and in the salvation that He has given us as a free gift. If the Lord Jesus truly is our delight and all that we desire on earth, it is not difficult to praise Him and to bless His Holy Name. From the time the sun rises, until it sets, the Lord is worthy of our praise (Psalm 113:3).

Like God's people in the Old Testament, we must go into battle declaring His greatness. It is with the praises of God in our mouths, and a double-edged sword in our hands, that we shall overcome our enemies. When eventually we arrive in heaven, we will stand around God's throne and be lost in wonder, love and praise.

## For reflection and action

*Live your life for the glory of God and give Him the praise that He deserves. It will cost you a lot to do this, but your sacrifice will be pleasing and acceptable to God.*

*Spend time daily considering all that God has done for you. Remember all His benefits and blessings. It is good and right to give thanks to the Lord.*

*Read and meditate on Psalm 148.*

**DAY 25**

# Obedient Thoughts

"... and we take captive every thought to make it obedient to Christ." 2 Corinthians 10:5

Our minds are a real battleground when we face long-term illness. There is a constant need to rule over our thinking. Our emotions, our will and our intellect are all somehow involved in the realm of the mind.

I find myself regularly thinking through the issues surrounding my life as a disabled person. The major thing that occupies my mind is my family. I am constantly aware of the pressure and demands which have been brought upon my wife by my illness. I have deep regrets about the fact that I cannot deal with the many practical things that need doing around the home. I regret, even more, the times when I give way to frustrations or fears because that only adds to my wife's burden. I have to capture thoughts about being useless and a burden. They will not solve any of the problems but only compound them.

I think also about my children and how much more I could have done for them and with them if I was fit and well. My heart aches as thoughts about the way my illness has affected them flood into my mind. I have to give all of those to God and steady my heart before His throne of grace. These are real battles, and I have had to win them in order to maintain a steady heart. It is only the grace of God that has enabled me to press on and not give way to despair.

The work I do as a full-time pastor in a church is another area of life that occupies a great part of my thinking. My mind is the all-important factor in my motivation to work, for it conditions my self-esteem and my ability to give myself positively to what God has called me to do. If I allow my thoughts to focus on the things I cannot do physically, it dampens my spirit and hinders me from achieving what I am capable of doing. My service for the Lord and His people is adversely affected. I have to take each negative and discouraging thought captive for the sake of Christ.

Your life, too, will be shaped by your thinking, not just mentally and emotionally, but spiritually as well. The enemy will target your mind specifically because if he can overpower you there, he can influence the whole of your life. Fears from within and without will rush upon us but we can resist them with God's help. If God is for us – and He is – then who can be against us? By His grace we can capture each invading thought and make it obedient to what the Lord wants. Our thinking and our lives will be shaped by God's Word and aligned to His perfect will. Our needs and desires will be less important than what the Lord wants and, like Paul, we will count everything in life as nothing compared to serving Him.

## For reflection and action

❧ *Allow God's Word to soak into your mind, thereby strengthening you to take captive every thought opposed to God and His will for your life.*

❧ *Read and meditate on Ephesians 6:12–18.*

**DAY 26**
# A Slave
# No More

"... and free those who all their lives were held in slavery by their fear of death." Hebrews 2:15

Humanity is enslaved by a fear of dying, but Jesus came to destroy the devil who holds the power of death. He totally defeated him and all the power of darkness by His work on the cross. Through Jesus we can be set free from that fear. For the Christian death has lost its sting and the grave is swallowed up in victory. If we are alive when Jesus returns, we will be caught up in the air to meet Him. If not, we will be raised up out of our graves. What a prospect!

In my own experience it is not easy to really take hold of this truth about death. It is wonderful, but it can still seem unreal and not somehow applicable to daily living. During my years of illness I have had to face the prospect of dying. The nearer I got to the possibility of leaving the scene of this life, the more fearful and panicky I seemed to get. I had to face up to the fact that I was terrified of dying.

I began to read passages of Scripture that speak about death and heaven. I spent time thinking my feelings through and asking the Lord to set me free from the terrible fear I was experiencing. Deep down I knew that things should be different. I wanted to know God's peace and to be confident about heaven and eternity.

Being very practical, I had to consciously align my thoughts and emotions to the truth of God's Word. I took hold of Paul's statement "to die is gain", and I allowed the Lord to make it a true revelation to my heart. I also began to think more about the reality of heaven. I had been living as if I belonged to this world and discovered that I had thought very little about the things above.

I prayed about my fears, I asked for God's help and for His peace, and I faced up to this awful monster called death. As I did so, I found that my fear began to grow less and my desire for heaven began to increase. The Lord began to give me greater insight into the futility of life without Him. Somehow, the whole experience seemed to clarify issues about life in this world and about the greatness of the salvation that we have through Jesus.

What a difference it makes when we are able to face illness without any fear of dying. It has nothing to do with merely adopting new concepts or ideas; we are not brainwashing ourselves. It is all to do with faith and the revelation of truth that God the Holy Spirit can bring to our hearts.

We can be confident about heaven and eternity. Nothing can separate us from God's love and we can look forward to being with the Lord and to receiving the crown of righteousness that is waiting for us in glory.

## For reflection and action

*Let me encourage you to break free from any fear of death. Don't be enslaved by it any more.*

*Take hold of the reality of heaven and don't allow the things of this world to have any hold on your heart.*

*Read and meditate on 1 Corinthians 15:20–26.*

**DAY 27**

# Handling Anger

"Get rid of all bitterness, rage and anger ..." Ephesians 4:31

From time to time, I have had to really battle with angry thoughts and feelings. Frustration and anger often come together, and when life is hard they will quickly dominate our hearts and minds if we allow them to. It is out of the abundance of the heart that our mouths speak, so anger within will inevitably gush out in talk which is unwholesome. It will not only be what we say that is bad, but also the way we say it.

Rash words are like sword-thrusts (Proverbs 12:18). People around us will be wounded and hurt, and those who are closest to us will be injured the most. Our attitudes and actions will also be affected. We will be aggressive and difficult to approach.

God's Word is very clear and specific about the whole question of anger. It tells us to put it away from us as far as possible (Colossians 3:8), and to deal with it quickly (Ephesians 4:26). If we don't handle our anger spiritually, it can open the door to sin. Like temptation, it is not essentially sinful in itself, but if yielded to it will lead to sinful actions.

I have heard lots of people refer to the incident in our Lord's life when He cleared the Temple of those who were trading there, and they cite this as an example of righteous anger. I believe it illustrates a holy zeal rather than anger (John 2:17). It was zeal for His Father's house that caused Jesus to go through that Temple like a whirlwind. He wasn't out of control or governed by angry thoughts, He knew that human anger does not achieve the righteousness of God.

If you have allowed yourself to be dominated by anger, you need to repent and to change bad habits.

Repentance is basically a change of mind, so your thinking must change first and then your life style will follow. True biblical change involves not only putting away things that are bad, but also starting to do things that are good. Let your anger be replaced by kindness and compassion. Don't only hate sin and wickedness, but also love and cherish righteousness. Let godly zeal replace human anger. Remember that it is good that overcomes evil (Romans 12:21).

The Holy Spirit will help you to work this important truth into your daily life; if you let Him. He will cause self-control and patience to develop in you more and more, and He will also enable you to change permanently rather than temporarily. He is the One who comes alongside to help us. It is by His power that we can put away anger and become like Jesus.

## For reflection and action

&. *Make sure that you put away anger as soon as you can. If you don't you will give Satan an opportunity to trip you up spiritually (Ephesians 4:27), and you will say and do things that you will regret.*

&. *Read and meditate on Ephesians 4:17–32.*

**DAY 28**

# Fragrant
# Garden

"A man reaps what he sows."

Galatians 6:7

The principle of sowing and reaping affects every area of our lives. According to the apostle Paul, we have a choice of fields to sow in, we can either sow to the Spirit, or alternatively, we can sow to the flesh. What we reap will be determined not only by where we sow, but what we sow. Every thought, every word and every action are like seeds that will germinate and eventually grow to yield a harvest. You can be certain that you will reap what you sow!

As we have already seen, we can sow seeds such as doubt and self-pity, or anger and complaining. One of the worst things that can take root in our hearts is bitterness (Hebrews 12:15). Those of us who are ill are vulnerable to this evil and poisonous seed, perhaps more than most. It will not only affect you in an adverse way, but inevitably it will damage others around you. Watch out for bitter thoughts or the early warning sign of resentment in your heart. Keep on receiving the abundant grace of God so that you can reign in life and sow continually to the Holy Spirit (Romans 5:17).

Being ill does not make us exempt from lustful thoughts or covetousness. We are not immune from jealousy or envy. We can still criticise others and allow pride to enter our hearts. Seeds like these will cause wicked and ungodly things to flow out of our lives. Be on your guard and keep sowing good, spiritual thoughts and actions.

I have had to learn a vital lesson since being ill. I must never use my illness as an excuse to sin. I have found myself at times excusing and justifying the bad seeds I have sown on the basis that I am ill. This is totally unacceptable. Just because you are ill, doesn't mean that you can speak or act the way you want. Neither does it follow that if you were well you would be fine. I've tried arguing that way myself! This illustrates exactly what the field of the flesh is like. It is full of self deception and wrong desires (James 1:14-15). If you sow in this way you will reap spiritual corruption and bondage.

Sometimes we sow very little and yet still expect to reap a lot. That's not how it works because God cannot be mocked! If you continually sow to your flesh, don't be surprised when you don't grow spiritually, or when you find that you have nothing solid to stand on during your illness. On the other hand, if you persist in sowing to the Spirit, you will reap a harvest of holiness and eternal rewards. Even having a sick body will not be able to hinder your spiritual growth and fruitfulness, the result of your faith and obedience will be an illness through which God is honoured and glorified.

## For reflection and action

*Your life can be like a secret garden, full of fragrance and beauty. If you sow to the Spirit, then His fruit will grow in you and your testimony will nourish and build up others. When people come into contact with you they will be blessed.*

*Read and meditate on Galatians 6:7-10.*

**DAY 29**

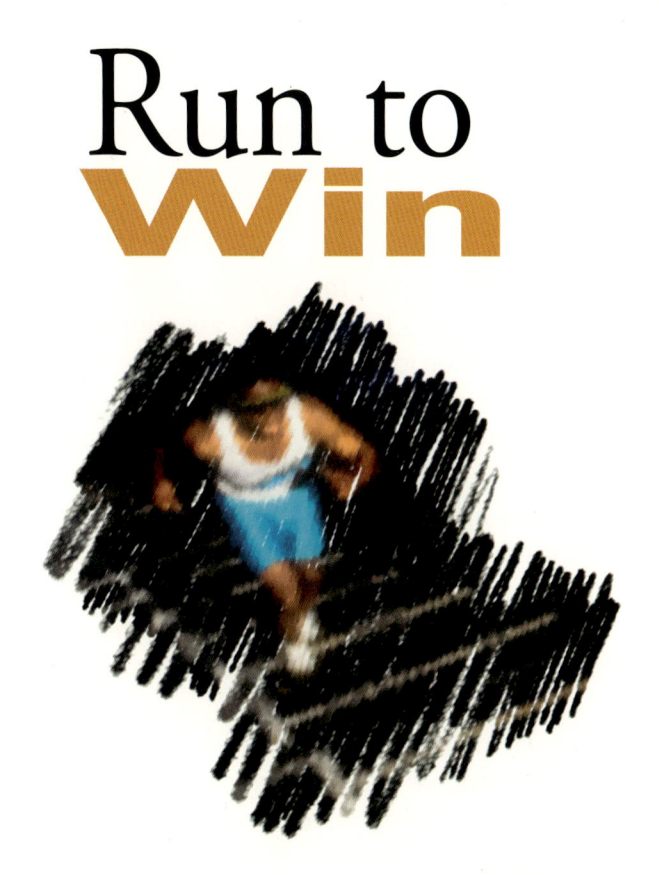

# Run to Win

"Never be lacking in zeal, but keep your spiritual fervour ... ."
Romans 12:11

In this evil world, and even in the midst of suffering, we can maintain a fervent spirit. If the Bible tells us to never lack something, you can be sure that it is possible to achieve it constantly. There are spiritual qualities which are still developing in us, some we have yet to attain, but others are in need of being maintained regularly, otherwise we can lose them.

The church in Ephesus, for example, didn't lose their first love for Jesus: they abandoned it (Revelation 2:4)! Our love for the Lord needs to be maintained and renewed daily and so does our zeal.

God wants us to be continually zealous for Him and His purposes. He wants us to be hot spiritually, not cold, and certainly not lukewarm (Revelation 3:16). Even during illness we can keep our spiritual fervour. Our spirit can be strong even when our body is weak. The power of God can be present in us and His strength can enable us to rise above our pain and suffering.

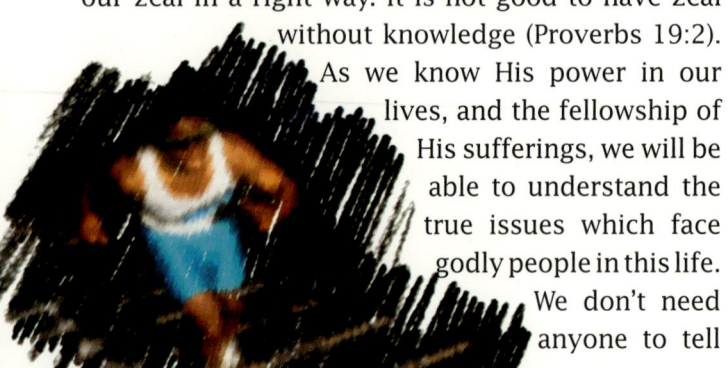

It is essential for us to know God's will and the truth of His Word, because this will cause us to direct our zeal in a right way. It is not good to have zeal without knowledge (Proverbs 19:2). As we know His power in our lives, and the fellowship of His sufferings, we will be able to understand the true issues which face godly people in this life. We don't need anyone to tell us how terrible sin is, or how wonderful heaven must be. Neither should we need to be reminded that living to please God on this earth is the best and most glorious thing that we can do. We can fix our gaze on the unseen and eternal realities which we know and possess in our precious Lord Jesus.

Let me encourage you to be zealous even though you are ill. Don't lose your fervency and spiritual vision. Be like Jesus, full of zeal for the Father's house. Pray zealously for God's people throughout the world. Pray for your local church and its leaders. Encourage fellow-believers that you meet. Impart faith and vision for the things of God and let the love of Jesus flow through you in any way possible.

Our God is a God of zeal. He has wrapped Himself in zeal like a cloak. He will achieve His purposes for the church and for each of His precious children.

## For reflection and action

❧ *You are not alone or forgotten; you are not a victim of fate and circumstances; neither are you without a future. You are a child of the King, and you have an eternal destiny.*

❧ *Keep on running the race and fighting the good fight with all your strength, for you are going to win, and receive a great reward which will last for ever and ever.*

❧ *Read and meditate on Isaiah 9:2–7.*

**DAY 30**

# No Earthly Reason

"Is anything too hard for the Lord?" Genesis 18:14

As we have looked at the spiritual principles that are needed to face long-term illness, you may have wondered if you are able to live by them. You may be under the illusion that only "special" people can cope spiritually with sickness and pain. You may feel totally inadequate to achieve the various things that we have looked at. If so, let me finish these studies by giving you the key to victorious Christian living.

God is able to work in you all the truths that we have studied. The power for living and for conquering is all of Him. Without Him you can do nothing. With Him you can do all things. He is able to do far more abundantly than you can even imagine. Nothing is too hard for the Lord!

When I was a student at Bible College many years ago, we had a saying: "Any old bush will do!" We would use it when talking about the ministry that we hoped one day to fulfil, or when talking jokingly about one another exercising Christian service. It was a reference to the burning bush that Moses saw in the wilderness. That was no special bush, it was very ordinary and just like any other. The thing that made it special was the fact that it had the fire of God in it!

It doesn't matter who you are, or how other people regard you in this world. Whether you are rich, poor, academically brilliant or not, what does matter is whether or not you are full of the Spirit and burning brightly for the glory of God!

The Lord has given us all that we need for life and godliness. The Holy Spirit teaches us all that we need to know and guides us into truth. We have the Word of

God and all the spiritual resources necessary to fulfil the purpose that has been planned for our lives. We also have a living hope for the future, and a place prepared for us in heaven. There is no excuse, and no earthly reason why we cannot succeed in achieving our potential as children of the living God. You can present yourself to God and live for Him no matter what this life, or the devil and his forces throw at you!

The darkness of illness will only make your light shine for God all the brighter. This victory over adversity, this strength in weakness, this joy in suffering, is not, after all, for us. It is for Him who bought us with His precious blood, the Lord Jesus Christ, who is our life and the One whom we love with all our hearts.

## For reflection and action

*Don't let illness rule your life; let Jesus rule your life!*

*Don't let the focus of attention be yourself, let it be Jesus. In everything give Him the pre-eminence and give Him all the glory.*

*Read and meditate on Ephesians 3:14–21.*